DISCERN
& DEPLOY
THE "HEIR"
FORCE

RELEASING THE SUPERNATURAL POWER OF GOD'S ANGELS

DR. CECILIA JACKSON

authorHOUSE®

AuthorHouse™
1663 Liberty Drive
Bloomington, IN 47403
www.authorhouse.com
Phone: 1 (800) 839-8640

Published by AuthorHouse 09/13/2017

ISBN: 978-1-5462-0572-2 (sc)
ISBN: 978-1-5462-0571-5 (e)

All Scriptures used are from King James Version.

Dedication

I extend special gratitude to my husband Dr. Michael Jackson, children, extended family, and friends for your prayers and support of this, and all other writing by "I AM" Fellowship Ministries, Inc. (Dr Jackson Speaks). I appreciate you.

Your counsel, patience, and encouragement have been such a blessing to me. I pray you reap double for what you have sown into my life.

Table of Contents

Foreword

Angels play a pivotal role in our lives. They are associated with nations, cities, villages, families, churches, and individuals. Angels are messengers set over our lives to help us and keep us from falling (Psalms 91).

We must be sensitive to their presence. When God says he will not leave nor forsake us, he is speaking about the innumerable angels that are working around the clock to protect us and make sure our needs are supplied. Although there are battles we engage in as humans, there are those that angels are fighting for us. As in the example in Daniel, there are those battles that only God and his angels can fight for us. These are our divine helpers to release, the hand of God in our lives

I've learned to expect angel assistance whenever I minister and in every place I minister. Usually the Lord will allow me to see angels present in situations. Once, we prayed and fought against principalities over our area; the Lord opened my eyes to see what angels looked like. Although the scene was horrifying, it was at the same time glorious to watch as the demonic enemies were chased out of our territory by the mighty power of the warrior angel armies of the Lord!!

I have experienced many divine encounters of intervention by God's mighty angelic forces, therefore I rejoice for the releasing of this book, *Discern and Deploy the "Heir" Force.* It is a comprehensive study tool to awaken and equip believers to understand and learn to access one of our most powerful weapons for victorious living -- the angelic hosts of the heavens!! Every believer, family, church, and ministry that is Kingdom minded would benefit from this book and be ushered into another realm of understanding the believer's availability for victory.

Apostle Mishael E. Rasou; Kwamhlanga South Africa

Preface

This book is written for personal study about understanding the reality and power of angelic beings who are assigned to help the believer with daily life. The work includes end of content questions and written assessment tools for personal or group discussion. In addition, the book is complete with declarations and prayers that can be spoken to activate angelic activity in the lives of believers.

The material's content is informational and informal as the author's intent is to reach a broad audience with what God wants to impart into his people while studying the subject matter, *Discern and Deploy the "Heir" Force*.

Scriptures are inserted to support information and thoughts. Some statements may be repeated for emphasis, and all scriptures are from the King James Version or paraphrased by the author.

The goal of the author is to effectively communicate the information, revelation, and instruction to Christians for the purpose of furthering Kingdom of God dominion during this present era. Furthermore, the goal is to inspire non-Christians to desire to know the Christ and Lord of the divine host of angels.

These are critical times and God is revealing to his servants around the globe what is needed for edifying believers and for the work of the ministry so we may believe and speak what the Word of God, the Bible, says. This unity is needed concerning the power God has released upon man through his angels, for daily victory. This understanding will propel his plan in the earth realm and equip the Church to reap the largest harvest of all times.

Introduction

Colossians 1:10 and 2:10 state Christ is the head power over every might, power, authority, principality, and dominion that exists. He is the pre-eminent one over all, both angelic and demonic powers.

There are demonic principalities and powers that are ruling over geographical areas and believers are instructed to bind these forces (Eph. 6:12) because God's power is greater and is the dominating force. While many ministries are called to teaching, preaching, and demonstrating in the area of deliverance; this work focuses on teaching, preaching and activating in the area of God's angelic force. It is important to know the role angels play in the lives of believers and to understand what the scriptures teach regarding these powerful beings. One of the most awesome benefits God has given His believers and His church is angelic help. Understanding the reality of your angelic support is necessary for daily, victorious Christian living and maintaining hope in the face of ongoing challenges.

The conditions on earth in the church, in communities and families, and the issues facing individuals; determine clearly that it is time to understand, acknowledge, discern, and know how to deploy the angelic forces assigned by God for our assistance. *Discern and Deploy the "Heir" Force.*

Chapter One

Clarification — Air / Heir

Homonyms are words that sound alike, but are spelled differently and have different meanings.

(Examples: sun/son -- stare/stair -- whale/wail -- toe/tow -- beet/beat---sale/sail --- hare/hair -- nose/knows)

Look carefully at these words saying aloud their pronunciations. Are there differences in the way they sound? No. The words in each pair sound exactly alike, but are spelled differently and have different meanings.

1) Air is defined: wind, breeze, draft, and movement of an element.
2) Heir is defined: One who receives an inheritance because of blood relationship; inheritance of land and property, power, influence, and valuable assets not necessarily labored for.

The blood of Jesus that redeemed us from sin causes the death spirit to pass over us and certifies us as heirs and joint heirs with God and Jesus Christ (Hebrews 1:14). We receive inheritances because of the shed blood of Jesus if we accept him as Lord. Doing so, we enter a covenant with God and receive benefits resulting from our covenant relationship with Jesus Christ. Some of the benefits are power, influence assets we have not necessarily labored for, and an army of angels who are assigned to help us through life.

This text is entitled *Discern and Deploy the "Heir" Force*. It is important for you to understand the value of knowing the power of this angelic force and the privilege of releasing the heir force of the Lord, which is the angelic assistance given to us, the heirs of salvation. To understand this, and all the themes of this book, one must have the foundational

1

understanding of the difference between the homonyms *air* and *heir.*

There are several parallels between the natural air force and our spiritual heir force. These parallels are taught in later sections of the book. You are now familiar with the difference between the homonyms *air* and *heir* and the meaning of *heir* force.

God's heavenly angels are the powerful beings that are on assignment to continually escort believers victoriously through life and to the fulfillment of our purpose for Kingdom dominion. They are the heir force.

Chapter Two
Angelic Warriors

Hebrews 12:22 states an innumerable company of angels assists us in having dominion over all things and all things are under our feet (Psalms 8:6). Revelations 12:4 confirms that only one third of the angels fell from heaven with Lucifer in rebellion against God; therefore two thirds of the angels that inhabit earth and earth's atmosphere are on our side! Far more angels are with us than against us!

Sometimes in the natural, we seem out-numbered in our quest to impact the world for the Kingdom of God, and even impact sometimes churches in the Kingdom that have need of renovation. Too often we see and hear so much negative activity that is happening locally, nationally, and internationally; but, the appointment of angelic warriors is good news.

It is important to understand that natural numbers are not equivalent to kingdom numbers. Kingdom numbers reflect winning in our favor, overwhelmingly. God is for us, the Holy Ghost is with us, Christ goes before us even as The Breaker. The Breaker, in scripture, was the Messiah who broke open the way and led his people (Micah 2:13). Likewise, the Lord will break through whatever is hindering us to lead the way. Millions of angels are standing in powerful force to implement and enforce the plans, laws and strategies of God, the Breaker. He will protect and impact resources and enforce the covenant made between us (the believer in Christ) and Him to do good for us!

More angels are in support of us than any other forces that may oppose us and fight against us, the believers. In II Kings 6 the Prophet Elisha and his servants were surrounded by the Syrian army and immensely outnumbered (in the natural) by war chariots and a powerful earthly army. Elisha's servant asked him what the strategy was in order to win in such a situation where they were naturally out-numbered. Elisha counseled his servant to calm down and remain composed. Furthermore, Elisha told the servant there were more who were on their side than who were opposing them.

The servant took a natural numerical count: 1, 2, 3 and was discomforted. Yet, Elisha prayed for the Lord to open his servant's eyes (his spiritual eyes) and to give him revelation and to breathe an open vision into his spirit and upon his eyes. This would transform his vision for a moment, shifting it from natural perception to seeing in the realm of the spirit world. The prayer was immediately answered. The servant looked upon the hillside and saw it was filled with God's army of angels, horses, chariots of fire, and many thousands of angels dressed for battle surrounding them! During that battle, God gave the victory in the face of overwhelming odds! Natural numbers do not compare to Kingdom numbers because the angelic forces are stationed and at attention for us as believers. They are equipped to war for us, and to win.

When Joshua was in position to conquer Jericho (Joshua 5:13-14) the scripture says he looked and saw a man standing opposite him with a sword in his hand. Joshua asked the man if he was on their side or if he was fighting for their opponents. The man said that he came as the captain of the hosts of the Lord. Then Joshua fell on his face to the earth and worshipped asking the Lord to say to his servant, Joshua what he wanted him to do.

Sources explain the word *host* in the Hebrew language to mean soldiers or warriors equipped for battle and organized for military service. Therefore, we can imply the man that Joshua referred to in the scripture was the leader of a huge, mass number of angelic beings, angelic soldiers or warriors equipped for battle. They were organized for military service. The angels were prepared and ready to help Joshua to conquer Jericho as they are positioned today to help us with our battles!

There is no difference for us, believers. Our angelic army is positioned, prepared, in military posture and ready to help us win any battle. They help us to conquer and defeat anything and anyone who rises up against us. It is for us to discern their presence in our lives and deploy them into service on our behalf.

There is a real organized army of God that functions as a military, fighting force for us. Inaccurate religious philosophies and displaced, false tradition, even family folklore have conditioned us to see angels as tiny children with wings who have little purpose or power. Or, we see them as gentle women in all white with white wings and halos who peacefully sing and play harps.

On the contrary, angels are warriors created and appointed by God to carry out His plans concerning us, the believers. Christ has commanded them to do so. We need to release them to their orders of deployment already given by Jesus Christ, to work on our behalf assisting us as the heirs of salvation. They already have their deployment paperwork from the pages of the Bible, from the Lord. So we are authorized to activate angels in our daily lives. We should align our visual and spiritual perception with God's word and experience the difference in our life as we deploy angels to intervene daily on our behalf.

Lord, today I pray, and I decree and declare that your people will see with greater discernment and realize with greater conviction that there is a spirit world where angels are waiting to serve on their behalf. Psalms 103:20 reads, praise the Lord you angels. You are strong and mighty ones who are assigned to execute the Lord's plans. You are listening to each of his commands.

The heavenly angels are real and they are organized in the heavens and ascend and descend upon earth in order to implement and expedite the plans of the Lord! They listen to each of the Lord's commands concerning us. Not only that, they set traps against the enemies of God and our enemies. This includes principalities, strong ones, dominions, powers, and rulers (2 Chronicles 20)! They help us win.

What, specifically, do angels do? They function comparable to other servants of earthly kings, yet they serve the redeemed believers of Christ in the Kingdom of God and carry out the orders of the King of the Kingdom of God. Angelic servants:

A) Guard and protect the King and his kingdom
B) Guard and protect the inhabitants of the Kingdom
C) Enforce the Kings reach /jurisdiction of authority
D) Patrol and Protect the borders and boundaries
E) Implement the King's strategies, peace, and laws
F) Steward over the King's resources which are the resources of the Kingdom
G) Facilitate and enforce covenants and the King's decrees
H) Keep weapons and warfare systems in functioning condition in order to carry out military orders
I) War against threats to the Kingdom
J) Assist and protect the King's family and heirs
K) Minister Fresh Fire of the Holy Ghost

ACTIVITY

So, what do angel warriors do? They function similar to the way other earthly servants do for their earthly kings and leaders. Discuss parallels of the facts above within the context of natural, earthly kings. Then read the list again within the context of the King of Glory and the Kingdom of God. You will notice similarities in events and actions that take place in kingdoms and the lives of its citizens both earthly and God's spiritual, supernatural Kingdom. It is written in scripture, the first man Adam was a living soul; the last Adam was a living spirit. Therefore what is spiritual did not come first, but the natural; and afterward the spiritual (1 Corinthians 15:45-46; 1 Corinthians 15:45). We can learn from some structural patterns of how earthly kingdoms are organized. This will help us understand the spiritual Kingdom in ways we can sometimes easier understand.

It is time to discern, perceive, and discover the presence of our angelic armies who are not weak little stout children with wings, nor gentle women in white dresses with halos; they are mighty, powerful beings, military agents with supernatural power and they are assigned by God to assist the heirs of salvation.

Furthermore, concerning angelic warriors and numbers; angelic forces of the Lord, the warrior angels, exponentially out-number the kingdom of darkness with supernatural power, strength, and intelligence in every area of combat: land, water, the core under the waters, and in the air.

Chapter Three
Angels in Scripture

1) **Hebrews 12:22 says we have come to the mountain called Sion, and to the city of the living God, the heavenly Jerusalem, and to an innumerable company of angels.**

Sion's original meaning (in the Hebrew) was a hill in Jerusalem. The meaning was figuratively and typologically the militant and triumphant Church of the Lord. We use the term *Zion* today.

In other words this holy scripture says we have inherited a militant, triumphant church, the city of the living God with a company of angels that cannot be counted who are fighting triumphantly on our behalf to accomplish the work of God's Kingdom and our purpose on earth.

Furthermore, creation is groaning for us to manifest that purpose. We are the answers to earth's problems and perplexities as we release the heir force to help us do his will.

Acknowledging and deploying the HEIR FORCE releases angelic hosts to do their job which is to win the wars in the heavens with and for us.

2) **Hebrews 1:13 states, "To which of the angels did he say at any time, 'Sit on my right hand, until I make thine enemies a footstool to be under your feet'?" Also, Hebrews 1:14 says the angels are all ministering spirits sent forth to minister for them who will be heirs of salvation (those who believe Jesus is both the Lord and Christ).**

These scriptures boast that God did not give angels the privilege to sit at his right hand, or the privilege to make their enemies obey and be a footstool under their feet. This was the authority given to his Son, Jesus Christ.

Following verse 13, God clarifies in verse 14 his order of government by saying the angels are ministering, serving, assisting spirits that he has sent forth to serve, help and support those who will be the future heirs of salvation. That means us, we who believe in the redemption plan.

The greatest days of the Church are not in the past; they are in the present and in the future. God intends the greatest harvest the world has known to come into his Kingdom. It will happen when we acknowledge and dispatch the heir force. It is our angelic force that takes authority over the air, the atmosphere, the earth, the marine world and every kingdom according to Ephesians 6. It is our inheritance to dispatch angelic forces to help us accomplish Kingdom destiny.

3) **Ephesians 6:12 states, "We wrestle not (alone) against flesh and blood, but against principalities, powers, rulers, of the darkness of this world, and spiritual wickedness in high places. So take the whole armor of God (which includes the heir force) that you can stand."**

Ephesians lists the weapons of warfare from man's perspective as he comes to God from the outer court of the Tabernacle of God progressing inward towards the Holy of Holies. But from the heavenly perspective of where we are today as Kingdom believers who are in Christ and in the New Covenant, we are reigning with Christ, and seated in heavenly places with him (Ephesians 2:6). Therefore, the Kingdom perspective and position of how we should look at our weapons is from the inside, the holy of holies, between the angels/Cherubim. Our view is looking from the mercy seat of God.

Understanding this fact, we realize our position is worshipping him where the presence of God is. In this position of mercy, we are surrounded by the cherubim (angels). This is early Old Testament symbolism that represents the New Covenant substance of the existence of the angelic heir force that dominates the land and the sea and every domain, thereby guaranteeing victory for the believer. Angels worship our God with us in the presence of the Lord just like the angels on the mercy seat in the holy of holies. The angels are part of our fighting and covering weapons in the army of the Lord, part of our whole armor. Just as the angels on the Ark of Covenant covered the presence of God and were fighting, protecting angels.

The outer court moving toward God contrasts the position from the presence of God, Holy of Holies, looking from the position of redemption. We are blood redeemed believers protected by the warring angels who are our helpers.

The contrasts are as follows:

- Kingdom Reigning vs. salvation only
- The Tabernacle of David / no separation from his presence vs. The Tabernacle of Moses / separations and restrictions
- Redemption by the blood of The Lamb Once vs. Atonement by a high priest / annual covering
- Freedom from Sin vs. Sins covered
- Victory in the Promised Land vs. Wandering in the Wilderness
- Angelic covering and protection wherever believers go .vs. Angelic covering and protection in one place where one man (the High Priest) can go

A full understanding of the armor in Ephesians 6:13 from the redemptive position in his presence, helps us to see how we, with the assistance of angelic hosts, have the power to stand during the evil days that crouch upon the earth. This truth brings more clarity to the following scriptures in Ephesians that tell us to stand. We better understand that greater is the Lord and his angels who are for us, than anything or anyone than can be against us.

More scriptures about angels (King James Bible or author paraphrased):

4) **Psalms 91:11: For he shall give <u>his angels</u> charge over thee, to keep thee in all thy ways.**

5) **Psalms 91:12: They (angels) shall bear thee up in their hands, lest thou dash thy foot against a stone.**

6) **Psalms 91:13: You will stomp upon the lion and snake: the young lion and the dragon (satan the fallen angels and Lucifer) you will stomp under feet in victory.**

7) **2 Kings 19: 34-36: For I will defend this city, to save it, for mine own sake, and for my servant David's sake. And it came to pass that night, that the angel of the LORD went out, and smote in the camp of the Assyrians 185,000 and when they arose early in the morning, behold, they *were* all dead corpses. So Sennacherib king of Assyria was pushed back, departed, and went and returned, and dwelt at Nineveh where he was.**

8) **Matthew 26:51-54: And, behold, one of them which were with Jesus stretched out his hand, and drew his sword, and struck a servant of the high priest's, and smote off his ear. Jesus to him, Put up your sword into his place: for all they that use the sword shall die with the sword. Know this, that I can now pray to my Father, and he will presently give me more than 12 legions of angels? But how then shall the scriptures be fulfilled that I will complete the plans of my Father in all things?**

How are we to understand the twelve legions of angels? In Christs' time Roman armies were divided into units:

8 men	=	1 unit
10 units (80 men)	=	1 century

6 centuries (480 men)	=	1 cohort
10 cohorts (4,800 men)	=	1 legion
5,280 soldiers	=	1 army
(12 legions	=	57,600)

Since one angel destroyed an army of 185,000 men in one night (II Kings 19), 57,600 angels (12 legions) could destroy 10 billion, 650 million (men, strong men, or evil forceat once. This is estimated as a little fewer than the number of men who live on planet earth now! Jesus said his Father could send enough angels to wipe out the majority of living beings on planet earth, or spiritual beings that inhabit the entire planet, earth!

Based on the fact that one-third of the angelic hosts followed Lucifer in his fall, two-thirds of angels remain. This means there are at least two angels working on our behalf for every opposing, fallen demon against us! So, one angle destroyed 185,000 of the enemies camp, thus our 2 angels can take out 370,000 evil forces against us! This gives fresh life to the scripture that says if God is for us, then who can stand against us. Hallelujah! Glory to the almighty God who was and is and is to come! Blessed be the Lord for he has given his angels charge over us!

9) **Hebrews 1:14 states, are not the angels all ministering servants sent out in the service of God for the assistance of those who inherit salvation?**

This final scripture listed is one of the most important scriptures that pertain to angels and believers. The angels are all servant creatures who are sent to assist those of us who are redeemed, born again by the blood of Jesus Christ. We are his heirs and because of salvation we have the benefits of having ministering angels for assistance. The word *charge* is also a military term, making Hebrews 1:14 very clear that the Lord has given his angels the military command to fight for every believer. *Discern and Deploy the Heir Force.*

Chapter Four
The Heir Force and Government

The angels are our <u>heir</u> force. Just as in the natural, the United States (U.S.) Government has an air force that has certain responsibilities; the spiritual government of the Kingdom of God has an heir force with responsibilities.

NATURAL CLARIFICATION and SPIRITUAL PARALLELS

Definition: The United States Air Force (USAF) is the aerial (airborne, moving) warfare service branch of the government of the United States Armed Forces. It is one of seven American uniformed services. It was initially part of the United States Army ground force. It supports the army, the navy, the marines, the reserves and the coastguard. The USAF was formed as a separate branch of the military on September 18th, 1947. It is the most recent branch of the U.S. military to be formed. It is a military service branch of air superiority, super exceptional warriors that serve their country.

When we parallel the natural USAF with the spiritual Kingdom's heir force, we must realize that it too, is a force of aerial warfare of the government of God. The heir force is superior, exceptional, and nonpareil in the supernatural realm. It is an armed, active force of superior warriors that works in conjunction with all the other partners in the Kingdom: worship, prayer, teaching, preaching, dance, banner, outreach, Bible study and fasting. All areas can be powerfully and exponentially impacted by we believers deploying hosts of God's angelic forces to assist them.

Ground level warfare services were not enough to deliver victory in battles for the natural U.S. government; therefore the USAF was separated into its own branch. Ground warfare in the Kingdom of God is not enough either. This means when we as mere mortals do warfare alone, we will have marginal victory at best in the realm of the spirit and supernatural world. Therefore, we must realize the presence of our angelic heir force and the need for reinforcement from this host of warriors who rule the air and can give us overwhelming victories. They are waiting for us to release them by speaking in faith that they exist, sincerely recognizing they are assigned to help us on our journey and expecting to see visible and applicable evidence of their assistance.

We can accomplish some things ground level (in the outer-courts of praise) but what is accomplished in the realm of the air (holy of holies, spirit, supernatural, the chambers of worship, the high heaven comes) from a superior warring power present in the atmosphere and released from the air to manifest on earth what we need from the Lord.

Our angels war in the air, the realm of the supernatural. They are the superior ability present in the atmosphere, even as we worship, dance, praise, teach, preach, pray, and study the word of God. They are doing our business as we ask the Lord to release them to do so. When released, they shift what occurs on earth to a place of alignment with the victory that is occurring in the heavens.

The main military duties and diplomacy of the U.S. Air Force is air supremacy which means superiority of the fighters in the air. This air superiority is the greatest degree of dominance whereas one force <u>paralyzes</u> the <u>conduct</u> behavior and operations of another on <u>land, sea, air</u>, and in <u>special operations forces.</u> This fighting branch is the innermost net-work of a military service. The U.S. Air Force can have this kind of impact at any given time and place without prohibitive interference, thus actively disarming any weaker force.

This is precisely what our heir force does for us. It's a powerful truth. Our angelic force is the greatest dominating force second only to Christ himself. It <u>paralyses the behavior of the enemy</u> (satan) and impacts change <u>on land, sea, air</u>, and even <u>dismantles the special services operations</u> of the enemies' plans against us and our loved ones. Our angels can have this impact at any given time and place without being prohibited, without interference. They can <u>disarm any weaker force</u>. Every other supernatural force is less powerful than these supernatural creatures who God assigned to assist us, the believers (Colossians 1:18 and 2:10). Re-read this explanation and think about it. Our heart and mind should be refreshed with hope and courage that we have help on our journey of life.

The enemy, Satan, does not have the ability to stop the heir force. Their special operations which are the assigned forces of darkness launched against us, our family, our church, our nation and the world for the Kingdom of God, are paralyzed and defeated in the atmosphere by God's heir force, our host of angelic warrior forces.

From the air (like the USAF), the angels, the heir force, dominate land, sea, air, and every intricate networking of the enemy force and paralyzes demonic forces. They make possible the present manifestation of what's already in eternity concerning our life on earth. We must regularly ask the Lord to release the angels on our behalf. He has actually already deployed them. They are waiting on us to agree they exist and release them to the service that they long to deliver to us. God has given them military charge over us to help us! They are our assistants!

The USAF articulates its core functions in twelve areas. A few are: <u>Global integration</u> and precision (no geographical limitations beyond their reach); <u>Cyberspace superiority</u> (dominates even in the virtual realm of cyber space, penetrates and has authority to impact computer generated activity); <u>Personnel Recovery</u> (whatever we need to be restored for our nation, our communities, jobs, infrastructure, whatever impacts Americans where the government is concerned); <u>Agile Ground Combat Support</u> (vigilant and skillful warriors who sabotage and defeat the enemy on ground as well).

Likewise, the believers heir force, the angelic hosts: <u>Have no limitation geographically or globally</u> and are <u>precise</u> in answering our requests (can come to our rescue no matter where we are); <u>Dominate cyberspace</u> (can even intervene in the virtual realm and can impact computer and satellite generated activity that is negative and/or destructive toward us or our loved ones); Can intervene in personal recovery (can help when we are disappointed, suffer loss, need obstacles moved in order to progress, need finances, health, anything impacting us personally); Dexterous, vigilant and skillful ground support (Angels help us with everyday tasks and challenges on our journey of life on earth and push us to destiny arrival). To understand the Kingdom governmental function of our heir force, re-read these categories above and meditate on them. We have help with our dreams, help with our plans, and help with our quest for a happy life. With God's heavenly host supporting us, we can enjoy life and peace in our lives personally, and make an impact for Christ in the Kingdom.

The U.S. Air Force is ultimately appointment by the President with Senate confirmation. Although they are assigned and directed by the Secretary of Defense, The Commander And Chief /President is the ultimate force behind the U.S. Air Force. Paralleling the natural, Jesus is the Captain of the hosts in charge of the angels that we acknowledge and dispatch. He is the Captain giving the orders for the angels to assist us and carry out requests on our behalf on earth. In Joshua 5:14 Jesus said as captain of the host of the Lord that he has come. Then Joshua fell on his face to the earth, and worshipped and asked the Lord what he wanted his servant to do. Scripturally, Christ as the captain of the hosts has already released them, so we must deploy them to the specific areas of our need, what we want them to do (Psalms 91:11, Luke 4:10-11, Hebrews 1:14, Psalms 34:7, Psalms 71:3).

Psalms 91:9 –12 is a word spoken concerning believers that parallels what was spoken to Jesus in Matthew 4:6 and Luke 4:11. It says when we make the Lord, the most high, our occupation and surrounding, spending time in his precious presence; no evil will happen to us and neither will any disease come near our living place because he gives his angels charge, custodial authority over us, to keep us in all we do. The angels will hold us in their hands, so even our foot won't be scraped by a stone. This is a promise.

Analogical Parallels

Similar to the U.S. Air Force, Our heir force functions in timely deployment to meet our needs.

The US Airforce	Our Heir Force
Works in concert with other functions	Works with other spiritual branches/ministries
Functions to preserve peace, security, defense	Preserves peace and security in our lives, families' lives, community, ministry, finances, church, and the Kingdom
Promotes national & global objectives	Serves us personally, but also has the greater objective of the nations and the Kingdom of God in all the earth
Overturns any aggressive nations who promote and carry out acts of peril, and purpose	Overturns any aggressive force that attempts to stop, or deplete the purpose of God's plan – no weapon formed ... shall prosper
Stated mission – to fly, and win in the air, space, and cyberspace superiority	Angels are in flight and positioned to war and win in every layer of our air space, and - cyberspace (casting down imaginations - every high thought) Angels have authority to impact virtual realm and dominate in cyber-crimes and technological cyber discovery

Global Integration and Precision	Angels have no geographical limitations; nothing is beyond their reach
Agile ground combat	Angels can assume many forms in order to help accomplish what we need on earth, even appear to human

Chapter Five
Angels and Destiny

A paramount function of our heir force is to help encourage and escort us to our destiny which enables us to do our part of manifesting as sons of God. Our individual calling and purpose on earth is important. Remember, angels are the most powerful force in the supernatural (other than the Lord Jesus) that work on our behalf. They help insure that we achieve our purpose on earth and bring us to fulfill destiny.

We have been in error and have allowed the angels of glory to be positioned as stand-byers, as we tirelessly navigate through some of the difficulty and the thicket of our life's journey. This dormancy has caused a greater groaning from creation for us, the sons of God to manifest our gifts and purpose on earth (Romans 8:22-24). We are to occupy (become active and visible) with authority and power over territory in our life and in our communities and churches for the Kingdom of God.

Angels help escort us to reach our destiny and establish his Kingdom in the world in greater measure than we have already seen. The Lord is sending forth a decree in our land for each of us to be in agreement with his plan, then we will see new and greater days of victory and triumph as the heir force fights, watches, supports and clears the debris from our pathway of achieving our divine purpose.

Creation is groaning for us, the sons of God and heirs of Christ to manifest (Romans 8:19). If we do not manifest our purpose and destiny in the earth, there will be no hope for the unbeliever, or for the church. We must engage ourselves, and teach future generations to engage in learning about and understanding the supernatural world and this benefit of releasing the heir force to supernaturally help us walk into full stature of our purpose and destiny.

Everyone has a mandate differing individually that must be carried out as we occupy until Jesus comes. Angels help us to accomplish that mandate.

In Matthew 18:10 Jesus encourages believers to be attentive that we do not dislike even one of his little children. He says in heaven their angels (plural – at least 2) always have access face to face with his father (God) who is in heaven and intervenes in the affairs of man employing angels to bring relief for us.

So, at least two angels are employed to bring relief on our behalf. Angels are already assigned to minister to believers. There is no scripture that says that we lose our angels as we become adults. Plus, there are billions of these guardian angels and there are millions of other angels who are busy following the commands of the Father assisting the believers, churches, and Kingdom work. They give us advantage over distractions and interference with achieving goals.

We limit them because of being unaware, unbelief, disobedience, sin, passivity, lack of knowledge and understanding, and our negative speech. Their purpose is to support us and our assignment for the Kingdom.

When we were in eternity existence before we were born, God already had a plan for our life. He was the first and only authentic author who wrote our life story. He wrote the thesis of our life before chronological time, created us in our mother's womb through the seed of our father and put us on earth to walk through our purpose. Part of our purpose is attached to our assignment contributing to the development of his Kingdom with our unique gifts and characteristics originally formed in us by God. There are angels assigned to help us achieve that unique purpose.

Remember, angels are constantly in the presence of God and have been, before we were born so they were made aware of our purpose by the author of our purpose, God the creator, the Lord Jesus the Son, and the Holy Spirit of God. So, before man's time began angels were anticipating our arrival, our birth on earth so they could be released to help us with all things concerning our life. They are ever waiting for a time to assist us into achieving our purpose. Remember angels announced the birth of Jesus in Bethlehem with a song, singing glory to the Lord in the highest and to men it would now be possible to live in full shalom, peace.

Second Timothy 1:9 states God has rescued us and authorized us with a holy calling, not according to our performance, but according to his **purpose** and dignity given to us in Christ Jesus before the world began. So before chronological time began, God rescued us and established our purpose and positioned angels to know and be available to be dispatched to assist us with accomplishing what he has given us the dignity to do.

The word *purpose* in ancient Greek is pro-theses. It means a proposal that is intentionally introduced as a course, a pathway, a sequence to our life. It is the debut and unveiling of a story, a narrative by God (our biography). It is paralleled to the bread on the Table of Showbread in the Temple as being a valuable life laid before the presence of God.

The root words *theses* and *thesis* mean the same. A theses is a proposition or proposal, a view, a dissertation, a paper, a composition or an essay. A thesis is likewise a proposition or proposal, an essay or paper, a plan or schematic structure of something. A written report, essay, or composition, dissertation or written schematic structure has to have a thesis statement. In fact, it is developed according to a thesis statement or clear focused topic. Every part of this thesis or theses is divided into paragraphs each guided by a topic sentence.

Then the message from Father, God in scripture from II Timothy means God of eternity: past, present, and future wrote our life's thesis statement and the narrative of our life intentionally, even before we were born. He wrote the schematic structure of our life before we were on earth. They were His plans for our life. Every paragraph has already been written. The very Godhead came together and contemplated, mulled over, pondered, deliberated over, consciously planned and pre-meditated what our life was to be and put us into our mother's womb (on earth) to carry out his plan from eternity past to present.

That's why the Lord says in Jeremiah 29:11 that he already knows the plans he has for us and those plans are for good and not for disaster, to give us a forthcoming, impending life with hope and an end that he expects us to walk out. Today, he still longs for us to cooperate with what he wrote concerning us.

Furthermore, the prefix *pro* means *before.* It also means professional as in a skilled authority, expert or specialist. Derivative words in our language are often parts of pieces of words called pre-fixes or pre-syllables to a root word. For example: pro-football player, pro-golf player, professional writer, professional talk show host, etc. Also, there are links to the syllable *pre* as in: preamble, preview, preface, preheat, and etcetera.

Accordingly, we further conclude that God, himself, existed in pre-chronological time and had us in his mind during pre-earth time and he is the ultimate of all professionals, so our story was written by *the* professional, not *a* professional. He is the writer of all writers, expert skilled above all others, the creator of heaven and earth. The angels were present and prepped, made aware of, their assignment to assist us whom he knew would become redeemed children of his and no one qualifies to edit anything He has written. Hallelujah!

Destiny – Scripture Support

1) **Luke, Chapter 1 - Zechariah, the high priest, and his wife Elizabeth were physically unable to bear children but barrenness was not their destiny.**

The angel of the Lord, Gabriel, appeared and revealed God's plan for their lives. It was their destiny to have a child who would be the prophet that would prepare the way for Jesus. The angel also knew John's destiny (their son) although he was not yet born. This was part of John's thesis and an angel of the Lord came on the scene to assist with the destiny of Zacharias, Elizabeth and John.

An angel appeared on the right side of the altar when Zacharias was praying and he was first afraid when he saw the angel.

> **Luke 1:13-15:** But **the angel** said unto him, Fear not, Zacharias: for thy prayer is heard; and thy wife Elisabeth shall bear thee a son, and you shall call his name John. And thou shalt have joy and gladness; and many shall rejoice at his birth. For he shall be great in the sight of the Lord, and shall drink neither wine nor strong drink; and he shall be filled with the Holy Ghost, even from his mother's womb. And many of the children of Israel shall he turn to the Lord their God

Customarily and traditionally, a Hebrew boy was named after his father. So, John should have been named Zacharias, after his father, but the words from the angel of the Lord were received by the high priest, Zacharias, giving him the confidence to carry out all of his purpose regarding the birth of his son. He named him John. This occurred after the angel had to strike him speechless because of his disbelief. Yet, the end result was the birthing of the purpose of God that would use John to shift a people, and the world for the present and the future.

> **Luke 1:18-19:** Zacharias said unto the angel, I am an old man, and my wife is stricken (negative view) because of aging years. The angel said unto him, I am Gabriel, standing in the presence of God; and am sent to speak to you to show you this good news. So you will not be able to speak until the day these things are performed, because you did not believe my words which will be fulfilled in their season.

2) **Luke, Chapter 1:30 - The angel Gabriel knew that Mary was to be the mother of Jesus. It was in the thesis of her destiny.**

The angel Gabriel actually revealed this to her and was there to help bring it to pass. He had already been briefed on her purpose in the presence of God, and gave her the courage to carry it out.

> **Luke 1:26:** The sixth month the angel Gabriel was sent from God unto a city named Nazareth to a virgin named Mary engaged to a man named Joseph.

> **Luke 1:28:** The angel said you are highly favored, the Lord *is* with you: you are blessed among women. She was disturbed and wondered what kind of greeting is this?

> **Luke 1:30:** The angel said, Fear not, Mary: you will conceive in your womb and have a son named Jesus who will be great, the Highest and of his kingdom there shall be no end.

> **Luke 1:34:** Mary, how will it happen, seeing I haven't slept with a man? He told her the power of the Holy Ghost would overshadow her and the child would be the Son of God.

> **Luke 1:37:** For with God nothing shall be impossible. Mary said...let it happen according to your word, and the angel left.

3) **Genesis, Chapter 24 - When it was time for Isaac, Abraham's son, to have a wife an angel knew Rebekah was in the destiny and purpose, already written in Isaac's thesis long before he knew it.**

An angel led Abraham's servant to her although she was in another country! The angel knew exactly where Rebekah was drawing water and connected the time and place and the persons for the thesis to be written. The destiny for Isaac was accomplished for Rebekah to be his wife. It prophetically progressed because of the intervention of an angel.

4) **Genesis, Chapter 32 – Jacob wrestled with an angel all night over his destiny. Even when we mess up, angels help us get back in position for fulfilling our destiny which is to complete the thesis written by God in eternity for us. <u>Angels are tenacious about helping the believers</u>. Jacob was a liar, deceiver, stole his brother's birthright, deceived his father and left his family for twenty years.**

It was an <u>angel of the Lord who appeared</u> to Jacob in a dream (Genesis 31:13) reminding him that he is the God of the house of God and to get up and return to his family.

5) **Judges, Chapter 6 - Gideon was at the bottom of the wine press beating the wheat grains from the stalks because he was afraid of the Midianite armies. For seven years, Israel's harvest had been stolen from them by Midianites terrorizing God's people, inflicting them with poverty, making them fearful, and causing them to hide in caves.**

But <u>the angel of the Lord knew Gideon's thesis</u>, his purpose, even when he did not know and was hiding in fear.

> **Judges 6:11:** There <u>came an angel of the LORD</u>, and appeared and sat under an oak where Gideon threshed wheat – and said to him – You mighty man of valor, the Lord is with you.

> **Judges 6:13-16:** Gideon <u>asked the angel questions</u> about the condition of Israel and the absence of miracles with them as was with their fathers. The LORD (who visits with angels) looked upon him, and said, go in this your might, and you will save Israel from the hand of the Midianites: I sent you. Gideon complained again about inability to help Israel because of the poverty

of his family – Manasseh. The LORD said unto him, for Certain I will be with you, and you will destroy the Midianites as one man.

Angels know about our abilities and are assigned to continually stir them up and connect you with kairos time and place which will unlock our anointing and release us into our destiny. Angels have been briefed on our destiny. We must release the heir force to assist us in reaching our destiny.

6) **Acts, 27 - The apostle Paul was a prisoner on a ship going to Italy when a violent storm arose. The ship was so tossed by the rainstorm that it was going to be destroyed. An angel intervened and stopped death by drowning.**

The <u>angel of the Lord appeared to Paul</u> (already knowing his thesis) and prepared to assist him telling him to not be fearful because it was in his destiny to be brought before Caesar. Because of Paul's obedience and prayer, angels were released to help him to his destiny even though they had to rescue him at sea.

> **Acts 27:22-24:** The angel told Paul that he had to get to Rome. The meaning in the Greek language strongly implied that it was unavoidable and Paul's obligation or appointment was that he had to get to Rome. In other words, Paul had been appointed by the divine creator for an assignment and <u>the angel was assuring him</u> that he would complete that destiny, the Lord's thesis for his life.

Destiny Conclusion

Creation is grumbling and moaning for the exhibitions and demonstrations of God's heirs, his children, his sons. It's time to release the heir force in our lives to support destiny's arrival of the story of our lives that God created before we were ever placed on earth.

Our heir force has global integration and precision which means there are no geographical limitations beyond their reach. Cyberspace superiority enables them to dominate even in the virtual realm penetrating and exercising authority to impact all these zones for Kingdom dominance and making space for our purpose. These angels intervene in personnel recovery to restore whatever losses incur while on the journey to reaching our destiny. Whether it's recovery for us, our children, our communities, finances, health, or anything; they qualify to help with whatever we do and need on earth to support destiny arrival.

Angel armies are with us and will get us to our Rome just as they did with Paul. Our heir force helps with divine appointments, escorts us to ordained places, watches over our seed and intervenes in generations, guides, leads, fights, destroys, comforts and cares, heals, and encourages. They are ministering and serving angels, public servants of the Kingdom government, agents sent forth to serve and assist those who are the heirs of salvation (Hebrews 1:14).

Yes, these angels have been briefed on our purpose therefore they open up the heavens, scatter and shatter powers of darkness aimed at us, and they empower, deliver and rescue believers and are appointed by God himself to enforce our safe arrival to destiny!

Chapter Six
The Nature of Angels

If we are to use our heir force to assist us, we must know of their nature and characteristics, their personality and mannerisms, also their background and experience.

God commissions angels to do many things for us. They have great value and worth. Let's look at a few general points, all of which could be topics resulting in pages of research. Yet, we'll gain enough understanding on each to be motivated for further personal study.

1) Angels are <u>intelligent, wise beings.</u> They are well aware of what is happening on earth. Another word for *wise* means they are cunning, clever and shrewd. They are not naive beings who were for yesterday; they are for us now. They are supernaturally wise; therefore they are aware of what takes place in all dimensions, not only aware of what happens on earth. II Samuel 14:20 compares the wisdom of the Lord to the wisdom of an angel of God who knows all things that exist in the earth.

2) Sometimes the rebellion and arrogance of mankind will cause an angel to react in a <u>wrathful manner</u>. When Herod dressed in royal apparel and accepted the praise and glory from the people as though he were God, an angel saw it and caused worms to attack his body until he died. Herod had provoked a protecting angel by not giving all glory to God. In this case the nurturing, caring nature of an angel shifted (Acts 12:20-23).

3) Another example of an angel being provoked is when Zacharias, who was a Jewish priest, was visited by an angel and told his aged wife, Elizabeth,

she would have a child. We would think the priest would rejoice and receive the word of the angel since they desperately wanted children. Instead, he questioned the angel (Gabriel) so Zacharias was punished by the angel with the inability to talk until the baby, John the Baptist, was born (Luke 1:12-19).

4) Our angels are motivated by our words of Faith. As we decree a thing (release wise, Godly pronouncements) the angels will assist in establishing these decrees. As we decide and decree in faith the word says it (that which we decree or deposit in the atmosphere will be established. Death and life are in the power of the tongue. Words of faith activate angels while unbelief stifles or represses and restrains them. We must agree with God's word at all times and his perspective for us and our families. We should not jolt and joggle our angels back and forth, but set them on a steady course to assist us with our needs. (See Job 22:28, Proverbs 18:21.)

5) Angels are assigned to help up on our journey to our purpose, but they cannot forgive sin. Only Christ can. In Exodus the people were going from slavery through the wilderness to the Promised Land. The Lord established a principal for us there. He said He was sending an angel before them to keep them and assist them in the ways of the Lord on their journey and to bring them into the place where he had prepared for them. In the same way, he has prepared a path and destiny for us. However, he gave them instructions to beware of the angel and obey his voice and God commanded them not to provoke the angel because he will not pardon transgressions/sin (Exodus 23:20-21). Only God can pardon and forgive sins. This divine action does not fall into the category of the assignment of angels.

6) Angels will cut off and destroy the enemy so we can prosper (Exodus 23:20-23). God says he will send an

angel before us where the wealth of the sinners has been stored up for us (Promised Land, destroying the Amorites, Hittites, Canaanites, etc.) He assured our prosperity back in the book of Exodus.

As far back as Genesis chapter 22 Abraham was told to take his son Isaac to the altar in the mountain and sacrifice him. Next, the Lord stopped him and told Abraham that He knew he feared God. Then, he showed that he had provided a substitute. Abraham named the place Jehovah Jireh, which means, the God who provides what we need. God provides for us all that we need. Not just salvation, but what we need to prosper as it is equivalent to how our soul is prospering (III John 1:2).

Also, angels connect us with prosperity as in Acts 10:4 when the Lord told Cornelius that his prayers and gifts to the poor had come before Him as a memorial. The word *memorial* means a reminder, or a record to rehearse something and bring to remembrance or attention a certain action or behavior. Cornelius' giving was in the discussion and remembrance around the throne of God. Therefore later, the Lord sent Peter to Cornelius' house and the Holy Spirit fell on all who were listening to the message. Everyone in Cornelius' house was saved and filled with the Holy Spirit!! That's prosperity!

7) **Angels strengthen and refresh us. When Elijah was running from Queen Jezebel and went to Beersheba and hid under a broom tree, he was exhausted and passed out there. An angel woke him up and gave him a baked cake and something to drink. He ate, drank, and then fell asleep again. This shows how tired the man of God was and how much he needed to be strengthened and refreshed. He was physically and emotionally exhausted. The angel made more cake and pulled from a well more water for him. The angel refreshed him again. This ministering and strengthening by the angel was necessary. It was so refreshing and fulfilling that that Elijah left and did not eat again for the next forty days and nights and he ran all the way to the mountain of**

God, Mount Horeb! He went from deep exhaustion to divine, supernatural strength!

The angels also ministered to Jesus and enabled him to finish his assignment after he had been severely tempted of the devil. The angels can be deployed to supernaturally minister to strength to us, energy, health, and inspiration. They are our heir force sent to help!

8) **Angels are more powerful than Lucifer and his demons**. Michael and his angels fought against Lucifer and his angels and God's angels won. Angels fight for God's people and they are victorious warriors!! They fight spiritual battles for us in the heavens when needed, whether the fight is over nations, regions, towns, social and cultural conditions, our economic needs, our health, our children, our ministries, our emotional condition, or keeping us from physical danger and more. Angels can also help us fight in the natural realm or the spiritual realm! [See: Revelations 12:7-11, 2 Kings 19:35 (185,000 soldiers killed), 2 Chronicles 20 (angels set ambush against the Moabite and Amorite armies that came to fight against God's people)].

9) **Angels assist in answering our prayers** (Daniel 9 & 10). (Acts 12:7-10), (Matthew 16:19).

10) **Angels protect and deliver God's people.** In Psalms 34:7 the word *deliver* means to rescue, paralleled to extending a victory. It also means to strip away chains, attachments (spiritual and natural). Peter was in a physical prison, but the angel of the Lord set him free. Angels can deliver and protect us from what is hindering us so we can maintain victory. When the Lord says angels, divine messengers, camp about us to deliver us, the early Hebrew language word was *encamp*. It meant to pitch a tent, set a siege for, or to set a watch for something. It

further meant to encircle us to set us free and to break chains that hold us. So just as demon spirits war to keep us bound, the angels of the Lord are surrounding us to deliver us, rescue us, strip away our bands that tie us to any type of sin or bondage, to watch for us, and set a siege (set a barricade, barrier, or blockade) on our behalf which ensures our victory.

11) **Angels work in the invisible and visible realm.** They also move at immense, accelerated speed on our behalf. They respond quickly. These powerful beings can appear as beings of light and even as mortal man and can go anywhere on earth in a moment's time. Light travels at approximately 180,000 miles per second. That's an amazing speed. Know that angels exceed this speed because their travel is enabled by the living God and exceeds all speed of mankind. This is how they can operate in our natural, visible world (bodily) and operate in the supernatural, invisible realm (celestial body). Hence, angels have the capacity to become physically involved in our lives if the need arises. Yet, they operate supernaturally in our spiritual world and assist us with their immense size and power in spiritual warfare. They can handle what we are not equipped to handling. Knowing that God has assigned this powerful company to serve us, the believers, is indicative of the love the Lord has for us! (See: Psalms 78:25, Numbers 22, John 20, Genesis 18:8 and 19:3, Revelations 8,9, Genesis 28:12, and Hebrews 13:2.)

This Section has presented a few of the voluminous facts about the nature, character and inclinations of angels. They are joyful beings, powerful and mighty, obedient to Father God, quick in response to their assignments to believers, holy, meek yet not weak, persistent, present to keep us company, the mouth of God to believers, give us warnings, they cover territories, assist with divine healing; and the list continues on and on. It is time to discern and deploy the heir force in your lives. Angels are waiting and anxious to do works of service for us.

Chapter Seven
Angels and Apostles

Angels are apostles have paralleling assignments. The Scripture in Hebrews 1:14 states angels are ministering spirits in the service of God and are deployed, positioned and commissioned to serve the heirs of God's salvation. This means those who have agreed that Jesus Christ is the Son of God and gave his life as a payment for the sins of man.

The Greek word for *angel* means *messenger*. In the Greek, the word *ministering* means to perform charitable deeds as a public servant does to help his country or government or a particular person in his government. The words *sent forth* in the Greek means they are distinguished and set apart. They have the liberty and are appointed to be sent out on a mission. Furthermore, they are sent from one place to another for employment and for doing business. Understanding this, we know angels are messengers set at liberty and sent from place to place to do the business of bringing relief. These powerful beings function and perform in love and warfare for the heirs of God's salvation! They are sent ones from God.

The Greek word for angels is the same derivative of the Greek word for *apostle*. This highlights that the work of the apostle and the ministry of angels flows together. They operate hand in hand. Apostles and angels are divinely sent to cover territories and to function for the work of the King of the Kingdom. Apostles are also called messengers. Their message is to fortify, establish, and build the Kingdom of God in sound doctrine and practices. Angels and apostles are linked.

Old Testament and New Testament Comparisons

The Hebrew word for angel means messenger; the same as the Greek word for angel. Both words refer to an ambassador who represents the one who sent him forth into the world. The one who sent him ahead into the world refers to the Lord Jesus Christ of the New Testament and God of the Old Testament This is true both for an angel and for an apostle.

Man in his need to control, thinks all apostles have to be sent forth by a man through the laying on of hands; while at the same time apostles are flowing in the anointing of the Lord all over the world as sent ones by the living God whom the Lord alone validated. They are not desirous of any title or documentation given by man, rather desiring the grace of God to do the work in and through them. Although it is good and nice to have man's recognition, the main documentation must be the calling and anointing of God to do the work. He sends forth apostles. When he endorses us, the power of signs and wonders will follow. Because of various world cultures and locations of people who place a demand for the anointing to fall upon them and their communities, Jesus will send empowered revelation of his word to hamlets, villages, mountains, and hillsides, communities, and far way places. He will appoint and send those who are willing to go to the harvest because the Lord is ultimately the one who sends. Sometimes we look for a man to send when we should look to the Lord. He appoints and sends the apostles as he appoints and sends angels.

The Hebrew word for angel also means one who is commissioned to perform a purpose for the living God and one who is ordained of God to complete that God-given purpose. In the Old Testament before the specific term *apostle* was used, the Hebrew word was translated to mean a prophet, priest, or teacher. Therefore, it refers to the New Testament work of the apostle as a prophet, Kingdom priest, or teacher who is sent by God. The ministry of apostles and angels flow together. Also, the term for *prophet* in the Old is synonymous with the term for prophet in the New. The term *priest* in the Old is synonymous with the term *pastor* in the New. The term *teacher* or rabbi in the Old refers to teacher today, which is one who moves about and teaches, such as an evangelist. Notice the link connecting the five-fold ministry gifts in the New

Testament to the Hebrew work for angel, in the Old Testament. God and his Word are amazing!

In the New Testament book of Revelation, the apostle John received a message from the Lord Jesus which was a message written to seven churches that were in Asia Minor. There were seven churches and seven regions specifically mentioned. Each letter began with words addressing the angel of the church (Revelations 2:1, 8, 12, 18; 3:1, 7, 14). So, the words from Jesus were to the apostles over the churches and the angels assigned to those regions. Angels assist apostles with the regions by which they have spiritual jurisdiction over. Just as there are hovering evil spirits over regions, there are ministering angel messengers assigned to bring relief and service over those ministries and individuals in those regions.

Both the Old and New Testament terminology parallel in explanation and revelation regarding angels, apostles, and the five-fold ministry gifts to the Body of Christ.

Apostles can feel secure in knowing that no matter where the areas are that God has sent them too, there are angel warriors assigned to assist them with accomplishing the goals of the Kingdom of God. Apostles must understand that just as they are sent, the angelic hosts are also sent with them to establish the Kingdom and the will of the King, Jesus, on earth as it is in heaven.

Chapter Eight
Angels and Healing

Heaven is releasing myriads of angels to do so much in the lives of Christ's believers. The writer of Hebrews says in verse 12:22 that we have come to mount Sion, and to the city of the living God, the heavenly Jerusalem, and to an innumerable company of angels.

One of the benefits the Lord has for us through our myriad of angels, the angelic heir force, is receiving healing through divine intervention. Angels cause breakthrough and establish the atmosphere for divine healing.

An angel stirred, agitated, and stimulated the pool of Bethesda in John 5:4, whoever got into the pool first would receive their healing. Although these angelic beings were released in Israel's ancient days to deliver healing to the people, we must understand that angels are present today when we pray for the sick whether it is prayer for others or praying privately for ourselves.

I had several experiences of angelic assistance in healing and angelic intervention for divine healing in my life. On a lovely spring day, my husband and I were shopping at Walmart. It was on a Saturday afternoon. Suddenly my right side started shutting down; eye, arm and leg movement delayed and horrendous pain. Within a few minutes I could not move my leg or arm without assistance. My husband helped me into the car and by the time we got to the emergency room I could barely see nor turn my head as it was pounding with excruciating pain. By the end of that night, after several tests, I received a diagnosis of an infection in the brain and was given potent medications to begin with and told further treatment would be determined after a team evaluated the symptoms and test results. When we asked about the paralysis, my husband and I were told that in some cases it goes away gradually and in other cases it lingers for quite some time or doesn't go away. For several weeks my husband had to help me from a wheelchair to the restroom and I was miserable as I drifted in and out of sleep due to the concentrated strength of medications.

This was during the time when I was working on my second master's degree and thanks to Michael (my husband) who was my academic advocate; I received an extension to complete the semester's course work later because of the medical emergency. I became singularly focused on what was going on in my body and what I was to do about it. I knew a life of sitting in a wheelchair unable to move my limbs was not for me. Furthermore, I did not want to become addicted to the pain medicines, anti-inflammatory medicines, steroids, and anti-biotics I was taking.

Each day we began creating an atmosphere for worship with music and the word of God. I am a worshipper so it was easy to mouth the words then begin to sing along with the recordings no matter how few of the words I could make sounds for. This created an atmosphere for the Presence of God, faith, and the company of angels to minister. The Lord spoke to my heart saying he had already given his angels *charge* over me to deliver me and heal by body, so to release them by speaking words of faith and they would intervene and alter my condition. Because of the atmosphere of worship and the word the Lord spoke to me, I built my faith, gained strength to open my spirit to the Holy Spirit and received what it meant to have the Lord give his angels custody, care, watch, control and supervision like guards covering and protecting me.

I began to declare that the angels of the Lord were guarding and shifting the intent of any evil forces against my body. I began to declare that the angels were with me with healing in their wings ministering to me as an heir of salvation. Through worship, the angels of the Lord delivered my breakthrough healing by shattering demonic resistance to God's purpose for my life.

God's angelic army altered a dismal attack of the enemy replacing it with total victory and healing for my body! The Lord Jesus used his angelic force, empowered and assigned by the Lord to assist me with my destiny, to minister to me during a time of personal need. This help is available to all believers.

Although the attack brought on fear, anxiety, disappointment, and hopelessness for the future, I obeyed the Lord and deployed the angels who were already on assignment for my life. In doing so, we welcomed their angelic presence and intervention. An environment of worship caused the Presence of the Lord to be fortified right there in my living room and my husband and I acknowledged God's Word concerning angels who are assigned to help the believers. The angels came and took custody of my physical condition bringing deliverance and total health as we decreed and declared, worshiped and deployed the heir force.

Within a week's time I was out of the wheel chair, the paralysis was gone. I could move every limb with ease, plus I could walk alone. The head pain was gone and the neck stiffness had subsided. I was back to a very different *normal* because of the experience I had with present day angelic assistance in the area of healing.

My confidence in the supernatural power of angelic forces was strengthened and my faith in God grew immensely because of the personal experience I had with angelic forces and a healing deliverance.

I also experienced visitation from an angel when I was given too much anesthesia during a surgery and loss consciousness to the extent that I could literally see my body on the operating table, as I was elevated in the spirit above the surgery scene in the operating room. I could see the doctors, the nurses, surgical technicians and assistants even the anesthesiologist sitting at the head of my bed monitoring me; but I could not speak. I only moved my head as I calmly and slowly watched and asked the Lord what was going on.

I then travelled down a dark tunnel experiencing the feeling of moving into a hollow place. Suddenly I saw a bright light and an angel who spoke to me telling me it was not time yet. "You must go back. There is much you're called to do and you are needed to help rear your children, especially your daughter". He even pulled back the shadow of darkness and showed me a house and the face and full stature of my daughter of whom I had not even given birth to. I did not know the gender of my child pre-delivery. I began to follow the angel and a light to the opening of the tunnel. When I awakened, I was in the recovery room.

When I came out of the surgery I stayed a few extra days in the hospital, but there was no temporary paralysis, no loss of brain activity, no organ impairment in any way and even my blood pressure was normal. God's angelic beings are available to assist us with healing and intervene when there is impending death. I was later told in consultation that my heart stopped on the operating table because my body responded abnormally to the anesthesia. I had come through, but it took much longer for the delivery because of other complications. The baby was fine.

I have experienced several other supernatural encounters that witness and proclaim the divine intervention of angelic hosts coming to the aid of a Christ follower. These many experiences confirm the reality of the warring, escorting, healing, caring, supporting, angelic army of God assigned to minister to the heirs of salvation. Angels intervened to escort me on my journey, making certain I reach my destiny and fulfill my purpose in life.

God has sent angelic reinforcement to earth to breakthrough barriers hindering our divine healing. They want to be active in our lives. We only need to discern their existence, acknowledge their presence and release them, deploy them in faith to do what Jesus has already assigned them to do in the area of healing and diving health.

Chapter Nine
Organization, Name, Rank

Angels are spoken of with different ranks and they function in an organizational structure and perform certain duties in Scripture.

1) Michael was called the chief prince.

Daniel 10:13: "But the prince of the kingdom of Persia withstood me one and twenty days: but, lo, Michael, one of the chief princes, came to help me; and I remained there with the kings of Persia."

Michael was called the archangel in Jude 9 and the great prince in Daniel 12:1, Michael is the only angel-designated archangel, and may possibly be the only one of this rank. One mission of the archangel was protector of Israel, protector of the church. Michael was to fight against Satan on the behalf of Israel in the Tribulation (Revelations 12:7–9). He is called Michael your prince in. Michael also disputed with Satan about the body of Moses (Jude 9).

2) Some angels are called Cherubim.

In Ezekiel 10:20, we are told that angels are cherubim. Cherubim are typically described in different forms as having two faces (also 4 faceand represented with wings, feet, and hands (Ezekiel 41:18 and Ezekiel 10:21). Cherubim were angels that guarded holy things such as the tree of life. In Genesis 3:24 God drove man out of the garden and placed Cherubim at the east of Eden. These angels swung flaming swords turning in all directions to protect the path to the tree of life. Cherubim were also seated covering over the Ark of the Covenant on the Mercy Seat in the Tabernacle of Moses and of David (1 Samuel 4:4 also see Exodus 26 and 2 Chronicles 3:7). In the building of the Tabernacle furniture, figures of Cherubim were embroidered on the veil of the Temple is Moses' Tabernacle (Psalms 80:1; 99:1). Solomon's temple also included Cherubim (1 Kings 6:26).

Read also Exodus 25:18-22 and Hebrews 9:5 for additional study on Cherubim. If you read this and other descriptions in Ezekiel 1:1-28, you will discover that real angels look nothing at all like cute, chubby babies with wings and halos and arrows. This was a pattern from ancient Greek mythology, the god cupid. Cherubim are of the highest order or class and were created with indescribable powers and beauty. They also had an unusual appearance with four face: a man, lion, ox, and an eagle. These angels had four wings and feet like a calf, shining like polished bronze. In the Holy of Holies in Moses' Tabernacle, Cherubim were protectors of God's glorious presence, his holiness, and his covenant.

3) Some angels are called Seraphim.

In Isaiah 6:1-8 we learn of the description of Seraphim. These are tall angels each with six wings and they can fly. The word *seraphim* (singular = seraph) means *fiery ones* and comes from the fire as associated with the Presence of God. They are also associated with praising God and called *the burning ones* because they represented the fire of God around his throne (Ezekiel 1:27, Isaiah 6:2-3).

4) Some angels are called Archangels.

Michael was referred to as the archangel and appears in 1 Thessalonians 4:16 and Jude 9. Gabriel, the archangel appears in both the Old and New Testament (OT / NT). In the OT Gabriel, an archangel is found in Daniel 8:15-26 and 9:21-27. In the NT he is mentioned in Luke 1:11-20 and 26-38. He is referred to as a messenger angel also. Michael the archangel is also referred to as a warrior angel who does battle (Daniel 10:13, 21; 12:1 and Revelations 12:7).

Gabriel's name means *man of God or God is strong*. Throughout scripture Gabriel seems to be God's special messenger of his kingdom program. He appears four times in the Bible record. He reveals and interprets God's purpose and program concerning the coming Messiah and his kingdom to the prophets and people of Israel. In Luke 1:26–27 Gabriel told Mary that the son who would be born to her would rule the throne of David. Gabriel also announced the birth of John the Baptist to Zacharias (Luke 1:11–20).

First Thessalonians 4:16 and 1 Peter 3:22 suggest there is a hierarchy of angels. For example: Scriptures speak of someone on the right side; some going into heaven, after angels and authorities and powers bow; the Lord coming from heaven with a shout and with the voice of the archangel and a trumpet of God, then the dead in Christ rising first. This all speaks of order and rank. Since we do not know all things, but only see in part, some of the revelation on angels is yet to be understood. Yet we do know these same angels are warriors and messengers for believers today. When the Lord gave angels charge over us, the believers, he did not say the charge excluded archangels. This means they are still our warriors and stand with us when we worship the Lord in his presence.

5) Some angels are called rulers or principalities.

These words are used seven times by Paul and indicate an order of angels (both good and evil) involved in governing the universe (Romans 8:38; Ephesians 1:21; 3:10; 6:12; Colossians 1:16; 2:10, 15). In other words, some were rulers and some were called principalities. They have authority over particular areas or regions in the world and in the atmosphere. This is part of the same angelic host that has authority in the air, land, sea, which means in space, cyberspace, and ground, everywhere. There is no geographical area that angels cannot rule over.

6) Some angels are called authorities or powers.

This highlights the superhuman authority of angels (and demons) exercised in relation to the affairs of the world

(Ephesians 1:21; 2:2; 3:10; 6:12; Colossians 1:16; 2:10, 15, 1 Peter 3:22; 2 Peter 2:11).

7) Some angels rule thrones or dominions.

This designation emphasizes the dignity and authority of angelic rulers in God's use of them in His government (Ephesians 1:21; Colossians 1:16; 2 Peter 2:10; Jude 8). These angels have authority over the affairs of governmental positions in the Kingdom. Today these angels help believers in the Kingdom with whatever their assignments are for the Lord.

8) Some angels are elect angels.

In 1 Timothy 5:21, Paul speaks of the elect angels. These are the holy angels who are somehow included in the elect purposes of God. These are angels who did not follow after Satan in his rebellion. There is little revealed about their election. Today, we only know they exist because the Word indicates they have an elect purpose of God. Since all angels are assigned to assist the heirs of salvation; they are still assigned to help us today.

9) Some are called the living creatures.

These are angelic creatures who seem to be involved with revealing the glory of the God of Israel in his omniscience, omnipotence, and omnipresence (Ezekiel 1:5-20; Revelations 4:6; 6:1). Ezekiel 10:15, 20 indicates they are cherubims. Through the four faces, they represent what God does to bring salvation to man through Jesus Christ: The face of the man suggests wisdom, compassion, intelligence and depicts Christ's humanity as the Son of man in Luke, possessing all these qualities while on earth; The face of a lion speaks of kingly appearance and pictures Christ as King as found in the lineage listed in Matthew, Christ the babe born who was the promised King of the Jews; The face of a bull or ox portrays a servant, the emphasis seen in Mark as Jesus the servant; as Christ the servant; The face of an eagle speaks of the deity of Christ the heavenly one, depicted in John's gospel account.

Paralleling this, today our angels have come to not only help reveal to the world the wisdom, compassion, and knowledge of the God of Israel through Christ, but to open the gateway for us to be able to walk in wisdom, compassion, and knowledge in every area possible. Our angels help reveal to the world who the King of the heavens and the earth really is (beyond, the God of Israel) to everyone. He is the King born a babe in a manger, but the King of the whole world. The angelic hosts enable us to witness to the world of the glory of the King of glory and to live in victory concerning all we are to receive as the heirs of the King. They battle on our behalf making it possible for us to receive all of our benefits as heirs of Christ. Relative to the face of the ox, the servant, angels are our servants since we are heirs to salvation. As the face of the eagle in Christ, we believers honor the deity of our King and we worship him. Our angels not only worship with us the Lord our King, but enable us to fulfill our calling assigned by our King to build and strengthen his kingdom.

10) Some angels are called watchers.

The early meaning of *Watchers* meant *vigilant, attentive, and observant.* Watchers are special types of angels who are constantly alert and prepared to serve the Lord and who watch over the rulers of the world and the affairs of men (Daniel 4:13, 17, 23). Our angelic army does this with pleasure. They know their assignment given them by God is to be attentive to our affairs on earth. Serving as watchers is their pleasure. They await our faith to recognize their presence and deploy them to serve us.

11) Some angels are associated with the tribulation.

A number of angels in the book of Revelation are specifically associated with specific judgments that will be poured out on the earth like the seven last plagues (Revelations 8-9; 16). In addition, some angels are connected to special functions given to them in these last days. There is the angel who has power over fire (Revelations 14:18), the angel of the waters (9:11), the angel of the abyss who will bind Satan (20:1-2). Although we may not understand all revelation with regard to the end times, we can be sure that we will need to deploy our heir force to support and fight for us during this period as well.

12) Some angels are associated with the Church.

In Revelations 2-3, each of the seven letters to the seven churches is addressed to the angel of that church. In the vision of chapter one (Revelations 1:16, 20), they each seem to be in the right hand of Christ in the vision. The term for angel means messenger, so we should consider that these letters refer to angelic beings who were in bodily form assisting the churches and their human leaders of the seven churches. Remember angels can take on a bodily, visible form if they need to. It's amazing to see the love of God that he would send angels to help churches. If leaders today would grab hold to this truth and realize there are angels available to help them today, we would see more churches growing, developing properly, unified, and moving in miracles and the manifesting power of God. It is necessary that churches discern and deploy the heir force. Our world today is in need of seeing the Glory. We need our angels on assignment to see the full manifestation of it.

13) Angels were assigned to assist in relation to new epochs of time. The same is true today.

Angels appear to be powerfully active when God initiates a new time period, a new move of His progressive revelations, a shift in what he is doing in the earth.

a. Angels joined in praise when the earth was created (Job 38:6-7).
b. They were involved in the giving of the Mosaic Law (Galatians 3:19, Hebrews 2:2).
c. They were active at the first announcement of Christ and to minister to him after being tempted by satan (Matthews 1:20, 4:11).
d. They were active during the early Days of the Church (Acts 8:26, 10:3, 7, 12:11).

 e. They will be involved in <u>events surrounding the Second Coming of Christ</u> (Matthew 25:31, 1 Thessalonians 4:1).

 f. The Spirit of God moved on a man named Martin Luther after the Dark Ages proclaiming the just shall live by faith.

 g. <u>Justification by faith</u> is restored to the Church.

 h. <u>Water Baptism</u> is restored through the Anabaptists.

 i. Emphasis on <u>holy living, fruitfulness</u> of the Christian live is restored. Powerful move of holiness.

 j. The <u>Holy Spirit Baptism</u> showered the earth.

 k. Gifts and the ministry of healing showered the earth.

 l. The ministry of the <u>Laying on of Hands</u> and Presbytery increased. Conferring of blessings to the believer

 m. Era of strong <u>teaching of the word of God</u>. A strong spiritual breath of God flowed upon the Church to seek and cry out for knowledge of God's Word.

 n. Restoration of the <u>five-fold ministry</u> understanding.

 o. Flow of the <u>Holy Spirit in worship and praise</u>.

 p. <u>Ministries of deliverance</u> were raised up.

 q. <u>Body of Christ ministry</u>, move of the saints.

 r. <u>Community out-reach</u>, church extension to world.

 s. <u>Foreign missions in ministry</u>, a church focus.

 t. <u>Young adults revival</u>, non-traditional concepts.

Since the ministry of angels occurred at other historical times, it is therefore biblical that this host of ministering angels continue to function in the present age of the church. We are the recipients of the prophetic word that a generation was coming that would be called the heirs of salvation and angels were appointed to minister to or serve that generation.

Hebrews 1:13 and 14 records the Lord asking a rhetorical question related to the fact that he did not ask an angel to sit on his right hand side until he made their enemies bow under their feet. He followed the question by saying angels are all ministering spirits that are sent forth to minister for them who will be heirs of salvation.

This is prophetic of the age in which we now live where these ranks of angles, this organized warrior force functions to serve the believer and God's Church. Angels did perform these ministries and continue to do so even though some are not aware of them nor their activities. This has been the problem. We have not been knowledgeable, aware or even convinced of their presence and their assignments to help us.

God does not have to use angels; he can do all these things directly with no help. But he chooses to employ the intermediary ministry of angels on many occasions. Nevertheless, the believer must recognize that it is the Lord who does these things whether directly or through angels. Notice Peter's testimony that the Lord delivered him from the prison although God actually used an angel to accomplish it, Acts 12:7-10 (compared with v. 11 and 17).

> **Act 12:7-9:** And, behold, the angel of the Lord came upon him, and a light shined in the prison: and he hit Peter on the side, and raised him up, saying, Get up quickly. And his chains fell off from his hands. And the angel said unto him, put your clothing on, and tie up thy sandals. And so he did. And he said to him, follow me. And he went out, and followed him; and believed that it was true which was done by the angel.

> **Act 12:17:** Peter beckoning unto them with the hand to hold their peace, declared unto them how the Lord had brought him out of the prison. And he said, Go show these things unto James, and to the brethren. And he departed, and went into another place.

God employs angels to assist believers in every epoch of time and will continue to do so.

14) Angels can appear in human form on earth.

> **Hebrews 13:1-2:** Let brotherly love continue. Be not forgetful to entertain strangers: for thereby some have entertained angels unawares.

Genesis 19:1: And there came two angels to Sodom at even; and Lot sat in the gate of Sodom: and Lot seeing them rose up to meet them; and he bowed himself with his face toward the ground.

15) Angels are called guardian angels.

The belief that every person has a specific guardian angel is from the statement that angels do guard or protect as Psalms 91:11 declares. But this passage is directed to those who make the Lord their refuge. The psalmist explained that no harm or disaster can happen to those who have made the Lord their refuge, their shelter from danger, because he has commissioned angels to care for them. This means angels protect us from physical harm and give believers strength to overcome difficulties.

Psalms 91:9-12: Because thou hast made the LORD, which is my refuge even the most High, thy habitation; there shall no evil befall thee, neither shall any plague come nigh thy dwelling. For he shall give his angels charge over thee, to keep thee in all thy ways. They shall bear thee up in *their* hands, lest thou dash thy foot against a stone.

Looking at Angelic Organization

While the Bible's revelation on the organization of angels is still being revealed, it is clear enough to show us there is definitely organization in the angelic world. They are organized into various positions, ranks and orders. This is suggested by the fact Michael is called the Archangel or chief angel (Jude 9). Daniel in Daniel 10:13 is called one of the chief princes. Ranks and orders are also suggested by the terms used for angels in Ephesians 3:10; 6:12, and 1 Peter 3:22, and others previously mentioned in this chapter.

The Scriptures are clear about the assembly, intervention, and council of angels (Psalms 89:5, 7), of their organization for battle (Revelations 12:7), and of a king over the demonic fallen angels (Revelations 9:11). Angels are also given governmental classifications which indicate organization and ranking (Ephesians 3:10, good angels; and Ephesians 6:12, evil angels). Unquestionably God has organized the heavenly, holy elect angels and Satan has organized the evil angels.

Angels are organized and believers must know they can't stand in victory alone or expect victory without understanding about the power and organized force of God's angels, especially since deploying this heir force is necessary for our well-being and success.

This Section has presented a few of the voluminous facts about the organization, rank, and various names of angels. Previously we have discovered some facts about nature, character and inclinations of angels. They are joyful beings, powerful and mighty, obedient to God, quick in response to their assignments to believers, holy, meek yet not weak, persistent, present to keep us company, the mouth of God to believers, give us warnings, they cover territories, assist with divine healings; and the list continues on and on. Angels in rank are waiting, organized and anxious to perform works of service for us.

Chapter Ten

Quick Facts Settling Common Questions

Although this is by no means a comprehensive list of facts and scriptures, it will contribute to building your faith in these marvelously beautiful and powerful beings that were created and are the servants to the heirs of salvation, the heir force.

1) Angels are spiritual beings.

Psalms 104:4: Who makes His angels spirits, His ministers a flame of fire.

Ephesians 3:10: To the intent that now the manifold wisdom of God might be made known by the church to the spiritual principalities and powers in the heavenly places.

2) Some angels are invisible.

Job 4:15: Then a spirit passed before my face; the hair of my flesh stood up.

Job 4:16: It stood still, but I could not discern the form thereof: an image was before mine eyes, there was silence, and I heard a voice, saying.

3) Angels were created to live for eternity.

Luke 20:36: Nor can they die anymore, for they are equal to the angels and are sons of God, being sons of the resurrection.

Revelations 4:8: Each of the four living creatures had six wings and was covered with eyes all around, even under his wings. Day and night they never stop saying: Holy, holy, holy is the Lord God Almighty who was, and is, and is to come.

4) Angels were present when God created the world.

Job 38:1-7: Then the LORD answered Job out of the storm. He said: "... Where were you when I laid the earth foundation? ... while the morning stars sang together and all the angels shouted for joy?"

5) Angels do not marry.

Matthew 22:30: At the resurrection people will neither marry nor be given in marriage; they will be like the angels in heaven.

6) Angels are too numerous to count.

Psalms 68:17: The chariots of God are tens of thousands and thousands of thousands.

Hebrews 12:22: But you have come to Mount Zion, to the heavenly Jerusalem, the city of the living God. You have come to thousands upon thousands of angels in joyful assembly.

7) Angels are wise and intelligent.

2 Samuel 14:17: Your maidservant said, 'The word of my lord the king will now be comforting; for as the angel of God, so is my lord the king in discerning good and evil. And may the LORD your God be with you.'

Daniel 9:21-22: While I was still in prayer, Gabriel, the man I had seen in the earlier vision, came to me in swift flight about the time of the evening sacrifice. He instructed me and said to me, "Daniel, I have now come to give you insight and understanding."

8) Angels have knowledge of, and interest in, the affairs of men.

Daniel 10:14: Now I have come to explain to you what will happen to your people in the future, for the vision concerns a time yet to come.

9) Angels are not meant to be worshiped.

Revelations 19:10: And I fell at his feet to worship him. But he said to me, "See that you do not do that! I am your fellow servant, and of your brethren who have the testimony of Jesus. Worship God! For the testimony of Jesus is the spirit of prophecy."

Revelations 22:8-9: "I, John, have heard and seen all these things. And when I finished hearing and seeing them, I fell down at the feet of the angel who had shown me these things, and I was about to worship him. But he said to me, "Don't do it! I am a servant together with you and with your brothers the prophets and of all those who obey the words in this book. Worship God!"

10) Angels have a will.

Isaiah 14:12-14: How art thou fallen from heaven, O Lucifer, son of the morning! *how* art thou cut down to the ground, which didst weaken the nations! For thou hast said in thine heart, I will ascend into heaven, I will exalt my throne above the stars of God: I will sit also upon the mount of the congregation, in the sides of the north. I will ascend above the heights of the clouds; I will be like the most High.

Luke 15:10: Likewise, I say to you, there is joy in the presence of the angels of God over one sinner who repents. (They willfully rejoice.)

11) Angels are faster than men.

Daniel 9:21: While I was still in prayer, Gabriel, the man I had seen in the earlier vision, came to me in swift flight about the time of the evening sacrifice.

Revelations 14:6: And I saw another angel flying through the sky, carrying the eternal Good News to proclaim to the people who belong to this world—to every nation, tribe, language, and people.

12) Angels can also eat physical food.

Psalms 78:25: Man did eat angels' food: he sent them meat to the full.

Genesis 18:1-2, 8: And the LORD appeared unto him in the plains of Mamre: and he sat in the tent door in the heat of the day. And he lift up his eyes and looked, and, lo, three men stood by him: and when he saw them, he ran to meet them from the tent door, and bowed himself toward the ground … And he took butter, and milk, and the calf which he had dressed, and set it before them; and he stood by them under the tree, and they did eat.

13) Angels possess superhuman strength.

Psalms 103:20: Bless the LORD, ye his angels, that excel in strength, that do his commandments, hearkening unto the voice of his word.

2 Thessalonians 1:7: And to you who are troubled rest with us, when the Lord Jesus shall be revealed from heaven with his mighty angels.

Revelations 18:21: And a mighty angel took up a stone like a great millstone, and cast it into the sea, saying, Thus with violence shall that great city Babylon be thrown down, and shall be found no more at all.

14) Angels are subject to Christ.

1 Peter 3:22: Who has gone into heaven and is at the right hand of God, angels and authorities and powers having been made subject to Him.

Jude 1:6: And the angels who did not keep their positions of authority but abandoned their own home—these he has kept in darkness, bound with everlasting chains for judgment on the great Day.

15) Angels express emotions like joy and longing.

Job 38:7: While the morning stars sang together and all the angels shouted for joy?

1 Peter 1:12: It was revealed to them that they were not serving themselves but you, when they spoke of the things that have now been told you by those who have preached the gospel to you by the Holy Spirit sent from heaven. Even angels long to look into these things.

16) Angels are not omnipresent, omnipotent or omniscient.

Daniel 10:12-13: Then he continued, Do not be afraid, Daniel. Since the first day that you set your mind to gain understanding and to humble yourself before your God, your words were heard, and I have come in response to them. But the prince of the Persian kingdom resisted me twenty-one days. Then Michael, one of the chief princes, came to help me, because I was detained there with the king of Persia.

Judges 1:9: Yet Michael the archangel, when contending with the devil he disputed about the body of Moses, durst not bring against him a railing accusation, but said, The Lord rebuke thee.

17) Most angels remained faithful to God.

Revelations 5:11-12: Then I looked and heard the voice of many angels, numbering thousands upon thousands, and ten thousand times ten thousand. They encircled the throne and the living creatures and the elders. In a loud voice they sang: Worthy is the Lamb, who was slain, to receive power and wealth and wisdom and strength and honor and glory and praise!

18) Angels have existed before the creation of man.

Job 38:4-8: Where wast thou when I laid the foundations of the earth? declare, if thou hast understanding. Who hath laid the measures thereof, if thou knowest? or who hath stretched the line upon it? Whereupon are the foundations thereof fastened? or who laid the corner stone thereof; When the morning stars sang together, and all the sons of God shouted for joy? Or *who* shut up the sea with doors, when it brake forth, as if it had issued out of the womb?

19) They are ministering spirits.

Hebrews 1:14: What are the angels, then? They are spirits who serve God and are sent by him to help those who are to receive salvation.

20) Angels have masculine gender.

Genesis 18:2: And he lifted up his eyes and looked, and, lo, three men stood by him: and when he saw them, he ran to meet them from the tent door, and bowed himself toward the ground.

21) Angels don't have sexual apparatus.

Luke 20:34-36: Jesus answered them, The men and women of this age marry, but the men and women who are worthy to rise from death and live in the age to come will not then marry. They will be like angels and cannot die.

22) Angels are immortal spirit beings.

Luke 20:34-36: Jesus answered them, The men and women of this age marry, but the men and women who are worthy to rise from death and live in the age to come will not then marry. They will be like angels and cannot die.

23) Angels are created beings.

Colossians 1:16-17: For by him were all things created, that are in heaven, and that are in earth, visible and invisible, whether they be thrones, or dominions, or principalities, or powers: all things were created by him, and for him: And he is before all things, and by him all things consist.

24) Angels are servants but not called children in God's family.

Hebrews 1:5: For God never said to any of his angels, You are my Son; today I have become your Father. Nor did God say about any angel, I will be his Father, and he will be my Son.

25) A third of the angels rebelled against God and are called demons.

Revelations 12:4: And his tail drew the third part of the stars of heaven, and did cast them to the earth.

James 2:19: Do you believe that there is only one God? Good! The demons also believe—and tremble with fear.

26) Rebellious angels are cast down to a certain hell.

2 Peter 2:4: For if God spared not the angels that sinned, but cast them down to hell, and delivered them into chains of darkness, to be reserved unto judgment...

Note: Hell in this verse is not the same hell that most people traditionally think of. According the foundational word, it means a place of restraint. Satan and his demons have been cast down to the earth and reserved until judgment. They are restrained, by the living God, and restricted to what powers they can exercise on earth toward man.

27) Angels may appear as human strangers.

Hebrews 13:2: Be not forgetful to entertain strangers: for thereby some have entertained angels unawares.

28) Humans cannot become angels.

John 3:13: And no man hath ascended up to heaven, but he that came down from heaven, even the Son of man which is in heaven.

29) Angels have different looks and appearances.

Isaiah 6:2: Around him flaming creatures were standing, each of which had six wings. Each creature covered its face with two wings, and its body with two, and used the other two for flying.

Note: Ezekiel 1:5-28 tells us more detailed information about what angels look like.

- They have four faces, four human hands, and four wings. Their legs are straight and don't bend. They have hoofs like those of a bull.
- They have human face in front, lion's face at the right, bull's face at the left, and an eagle's face at the back.
- They move with a speed of lighting.
- On their heads is a dome of dazzling crystal.
- The sound of their wings is like the sound of the roaring sea, noise of a huge army, and the voice of God.
- Brilliant light.
- Having six wings
- In human-like form
- In a combination of man, beast, and birds
- They never appear as old men because they neither age nor die.
- Able to fly.

Note: It is true that some angels might have an out-of-this-world appearance. This explains why, in the Bible, we have seen men who fell down in great fear when they see angels. Angels can also take the human form or other forms since they are spirit beings. Angels might have different appearances that we don't know of yet and has never been described.

Since they are spirit beings, they are usually not seen, unless God gives the ability to see them or unless they manifest themselves. Balaam could not see the angel standing in his way until the Lord opened his eyes (Numbers 22:31) and Elisha's servant could not see the host of angels surrounding him until Elisha prayed for his eyes to be opened (2 Kings 6:17).

There is little indication of angels appearing in female form. While angels generally appear as men in Scripture, this is not always the case. The two women mentioned in this passage, Zechariah 5:9, are not specifically called angels, but they are clearly agents of God.

See the following scriptures with reference to how angels look: Genesis 18:2, 16, 22; Genesis 19:1, 5, 10, 12, 15, 16; Judges 13:6; Mark 16:5; Luke 24:4; Luke 2:9; 9:26; Matthew 28:3; John 20:12; Acts 1:10; Ezekiel 1:13; Daniel 10:6; Ezekiel 1:5; Isaiah 6:6; and Luke 20:36.

30) There are over a million angels.

Daniel 7:10: A fiery stream issued and came forth from before Him. A thousand thousands ministered to Him; Ten thousand times ten thousand stood before Him. The court was seated, and the books were opened.

Hebrews 12:22: But ye are come unto mount Sion, and unto the city of the living God, the heavenly Jerusalem, and to an innumerable company of angels.

Matthew 26:53: Thinkest thou that I cannot now pray to my Father, and he shall presently give me more than twelve legions of angels.

31) Angels can protect humans from danger.

Psalms 34:7: The angel of the LORD encamps all around those who fear Him, and delivers them.

32) Evil angels or demons can transform as angels of light.

2 Corinthians 11:14: And no marvel; for Satan himself is transformed into an angel of light.

Note: The traditional depiction of Satan is deceiving. If he would like to deceive a person, he will never appear as a scary, red, and hairy man with pointed horns and tails and a pitchfork. So we need to be cautious because demons and Satan can also appear as angels of light.

33) Angels were created to glorify and worship God the Father and God the Son.

Revelations 4:8, Hebrews 1:6

34) Angels report to God.

Job 1:6, Job 2:1

35) Angels observe God's people.

Luke 12:8-9, 1 Corinthians 4:9, 1 Timothy 5:21.

36) Angels announced the birth of Jesus.

Luke 2:10-14

37) Angels perform the will of God.

Psalms 104:4

38) Angels ministered to Jesus.

Matthew 4:11, Luke 22:43

39) Angels help humans.

Hebrews 1:14

40) Angels rejoice in God's work of creation.

Job 38:1-7, Revelations 4:11

41) Angels rejoice in God's work of salvation.

Luke 15:10

42) Angels will join believers in the heavenly kingdom. Hebrews 12:22-23

43) Angels are ministers in God's spiritual service.

44) Angels are messengers.

45) Angels are watchers or overseers for God.

46) Angels are military hosts - assigned to war.

47) Angels are sons of the mighty, sons of God.

48) Some angels have names in the Bible.

Daniel 8:16, Luke 1:19, Luke 1:26

49) Satan's demons can appear as angels of light.

2 Corinthians 11:14: And no marvel; for Satan himself is transformed into an angel of light. (also, see Luke 10:18)

Chapter Eleven
Exhortation -- Pass it On

One of greatest God-given, Kingdom mandates to us is to pass on to our seed and the next generation an understanding of the power of the supernatural / spiritual realm. It is really the force that rules Earth realm, and this ruling is expedited from another dimension which is the spirit / supernatural world. It is the heavens and the Throne of God in Eternity World. If we do not exercise and teach our seed and spiritual children, the future generations, to understand and learn to dominate in the supernatural world; they will be dominated!

You might say, they can't even dominate their natural and everyday world. I say you're wearing your "carnal" thinking hat. Pull it off; snatch it off and begin to allow restoration of your spirit man. Then you will understand that if we can teach our seed to be aware of and dominate the spirit realm and the supernatural, they will have no problem dominating the earth/natural/carnal realm.

Part of understanding and exercising the supernatural is to know how to acknowledge and dispatch the angelic heir force.

I'm praying, decreeing, and releasing the heir force over your lives as I write this chapter encouraging you to motivate your children and generations of the spiritual children you have birthed in Christ. They must come to a greater level of maturity in the knowledge of the truths in this book. I decree and declare that you will pass your understanding on to them.

WHY? Creation is groaning for you, the sons of God and heirs of Christ to manifest and develop in your purpose and reach your divine destiny. If you do not manifest your purpose and destiny in the earth, there will be no hope for the unbeliever, or for the church.

We know we have the ability to totally change what is occurring in our earth world today. Our mandate is to be the light in this darkness and to compel and usher as many as we can into the Kingdom of God also to impact the believers to grow up and manifest the work of the ministry given to them on earth. So everyone has a mandate differing individually that must be carried out as we militaristically occupy until Jesus returns and dominates with Kingdom authority. Without the supernatural intervention of angelic hosts this cannot happen. Let this book be an inspiration to activate you to take action by faith to discern and deploy the heir force for yourself and your seed.

Chapter Twelve

Declarations, Angelic Decrees and Prayers

1) Father, release upon earth the armies of angels you have ordained to assist us during these time.
2) Loose your angel armies to battle against fallen demons and battle for us.
3) We decree the powers, rulers, and dominions of hell will be shaken from their positions of influence.
4) We decree and declare the righteous will prevail and the Word of the Lord will not return void when we speak.
5) Lord, assist us in rising to occupy the throne of our region.
6) We decree the heirs, seated with Christ in heavenly places occupy the territorial thrones of this region.
7) In Jesus' name, we cleanse the heavens over our region of principalities and powers of darkness.
8) We decree the church of God, the ecclesia, rules over and overrules the kingdom of hell, in Jesus' name and we establish the Kingdom of God.
9) We declare that the angels are protecting us, delivering us, and enforcing our belief in the Word of God and His prophets.
10) We decree the help of angels to assist us in penetrating and impacting oppressive government local, nationally, and internationally.
11) We release our angelic help and loose them to assist us in purpose, assignment and destiny.
12) We discern the presence of angels and dispatch them to move with power to bring all of God's Word to pass concerning our lives.
13) We declare that angels are listening and hasten to answer our prayers as they align with the purpose of God.

14) We discern the presence of angels and decree and declare that they are listening to the prophetic words we speak and those spoken from true prophets, and they hasten to assist those words to manifestation.

15) We discern the presence of angels to assist, help, comfort, and lead our children and children's children in generations to come.

16) We declare the angels are assisting to cause America to be on fire with revival, and the nations to increase in the fire of revival.

17) We discern and rejoice that the angels are surrounding, orbiting us to help in every area of our lives.

18) We decree we will "stand" in the covenant and authority of the Lord and appoint angels to war and lead us to victory.

19) We declare angels will assist in gathering the greatest harvest the world has known.

20) We decree new things being done in this new season.

21) We declare that Angels who assist apostles, prophets, pastors, and evangelists, and teachers shift regions, be released to the servants of God.

22) We decree that appointed messengers are with us to escort us to complete apostolic assignments.

23) We discern and deploy angel warriors to arrest and bind spirits that rule in our nation, the United States and other nations around the globe.

24) We decree and declare that angels will assist believers with their assignments by bringing down and rendering useless spirits that bind systems, institutions, families, communities, and individuals.

25) We decree and declare that angels will strengthen the Lord's church (the ecclesia) throughout the world.

26) We decree and declare that angels are released to assist in the trans-generational outpouring prophesied by Joel upon us in this era, it is for us today.

27) We discern and dispatch angels who attack Ahabs, Absaloms, and Jezebels in regions of our nation and the world.

28) We dispatch angel armies to break through the atmosphere so the Spirit of the Lord will minister to us a greater measure of words of wisdom, words of knowledge, gifts of healing, working of miracles, gifts of utterance (prophecy tongues interpretation), gifts of faith, and discerning of spirits.

29) We loose the angels to drape us with mantles of power for new beginnings as they encamp around us because we fear and love the Lord.

30) We declare and decree that angels go before us and are releasing restoration of our resources, and they are being multiplied.

31) We pray and declare that angels will arrange divine connections to people, events, and places for Kingdom glory and dominion.

32) We declare angel activity is increasing exponentially on planet earth.

33) We pray and declare a holy alignment of remnant believers with heaven's armies of angels that will supernaturally impact the coming generation.

34) We declare and decree that angels of the Lord are ambushing hell's forces as our praise and worship ascends like incense before the King upon His throne.

35) We decree and declare in prayer and righteous proclamation that all these declarations and decrees spoken and those we will add to this list will set a blaze of the Anointing and the Fire of God that will impact the epicenter of the kingdom of darkness and inject the Presence of the Lord that will shift us, our families, the church, and the nations, and generations from: hell's delusions, mediocrity, oppression, complacency, and from doctrines of devils. We decree this Anointing ablaze will shift us to: glory, strength, power, and fresh vision that will support and empower the destiny of every believer to completion of manifestation as sons of God -- which will render the work of the evil one useless and the Kingdom of God reigning in dominion in the earth. **Amen!**

Conclusion

These are critical times and God is revealing to his servants around the globe, what is needed for the work of the ministry during this unique era so we may speak the same thing, believe the same thing, and walk in the unity that will propel his plan In the earth realm and equip believers to reap the largest harvest of all times. Understanding angels, the believers Heir Force, is part of this equipping. Although this material is presented in basic truth form, it is a powerful thrust forward into Kingdom dominion and the present victory available to the believer.

The conditions on earth, in nations, in the churches, in communities and families, and the issues facing individuals all determine clearly that it is time to understand, acknowledge, discern, and know how to deploy the angelic forces assigned by God for our assistance – Discern and Deploy the Heir Force!

Questions/Evaluation

(Chapters 1 – 4, Chapters 5 – 8, Chapters 9 – 12)

Questions /Evaluation
Sections 1 – 4 (Answer true or false.)

1) ____ An heir receives an inheritance because of blood relationship.
2) ____ Heirs means receivers of healing, primarily.
3) _____ Kingdom numbers are exponentially larger than regular numbers.
4) _____ Prayer caused the eyes of Elisha's servant to be opened.
5) _____ A servant saw angel armies, horses and chariots of fire protecting the believer at a time of war.
6) _____ Angels seldom patrol boarders.
7) _____ Angels enforce the jurisdiction of authority in our lives.
8) _____ Believers have come into access of an innumerable company of angels waiting to be deployed to support them.
9) _____ Creation longs for a believer to manifest his/her purpose.
10)_____ Hebrews 1:13 says angels are helping, ministering spirits.
11)_____ Angelic warriors are part of the whole armor of God.
12)_____ Our covenant calls for us to approach God from the perspective of the Holy of Holies, the heavenly/angelic view.
13)_____ There is a difference between salvation and Kingdom reigning.
14)_____ God says he has given his angels custody over us believers.
15)_____ There is a difference between atonement and redemption.

16)_____ The angels help us have victory over servant-like people and those who are like the young lion and dragon in nature.

17)_____ An angel of the Lord killed 185,000 Assyrian enemies in one night's battle

18)_____ There are 2/3rd's angelic hosts that remain faithful to the Lord.

19)_____ It is not wise to expose our seed and young believers to supernatural truths regarding the spiritual realm.

20)_____ If a person dominates in the spiritual realm, they will dominate in the natural realm.

21)_____ One of the greatest Kingdom mandates is to pass on to our seed and the next generation an understanding and value for the supernatural in Christ.

22)_____ Our days on earth will be increased and the days of our children, if we remember to put the Word in their heart and soul and teach them while they are younger.

Questions /Evaluation
Sections 5 – 8 (Respond to the Following.)

1) How do angels help with achieving destiny?
2) The USAF is a military service branch with air superiority. Connect this natural fact to the function of the *Heir* Force.
3) At one time the USAF was part of the ground warfare branch of the military until they were separated into their own branch. Why do you suppose it was necessary to separate and strengthen the air force?
4) Discuss this reasoning with the need to have an *Heir* force although the Kingdom has prayer, worship, preaching, study of the word, and other ministries.
5) The Air Force is the branch that paralyzes the conduct and operations on land, sea, air and in special operations forces (the most hidden plans of warfare). Explain the analogy as it refers to the *Heir* force and its power to paralyze the enemy in all areas.

6) Explain the unique way that angels can present assistance in order to help us accomplish what we need on earth.
7) Explain a Biblical example of an angel being wrathful.
8) Why can't angels forgive sin?
9) How can an angel help us to prosper?
10) How was a man of God strengthened and refreshed by an angel?
11) Discuss some facts about cherubim angels.
12) Explain some characteristics about archangels.
13) Name at least six kinds of angels.
14) Explain who wrote your thesis before time on earth began.
15) Explain two examples of angels being present when one's future was concerned.
16) Tell at least one person in your class about an encounter with an angle that supported a Biblical character to destiny.
17) Explain how you will allow the angels to be deployed to assist you with your plans for the future.

Questions /Evaluation

Sections 9 – 12 (Answer yes or no/ true or false to the following)

1) ____ Is heaven releasing myriads of angels to serve the believer?
2) ____ An angel once caused waters from a pool to heal the first one who stepped into the pool.
3) ____ Can worship create an atmosphere for angels to operate?
4) ____ The word for *custody* with regard to angels means control and supervision.
5) ____ The Hebrew word for angel is apostle.
6) ____ The Hebrew word for angel is one who is commissioned to perform a purpose for the living God.
7) ____ Each of the seven Churches in the New Testament received letters addressed from apostles of that day.

8) ____ No matter where God sends apostles, the angels warriors assist them with accomplishing the goals for the Kingdom of God.

9) ____ Angels are not spiritual beings.

10) ____ Some angels are invisible.

11) ____ Angels cannot die, but live throughout eternity.

12) ____ Angels were present when God created the world.

13) ____ Angels can marry after many generations.

14) ____ Angels are obedient, but not very intelligent.

15) ____ Do angels have a will?

16) ____ What kind of strength do angels have?

17) ____ Can angels eat physical food?

18) ____ Angels can express emotions.

19) ____ Angels were in existence before man was.

20) ____ Angels are typically of masculine gender.

21) ____ Can humans transition to become angels?

22) ____ Angels can look frightening.

23) ____ Angels are meant to be worshipped for their labor.

24) ____ We are to pray and make declarations regarding angels and their function in our lives, in the lives of our families, communities, nation and in the world.

25) For the next evaluations (25 – 30), write five declarations, prayers, or decrees regarding angelic beings.

Bibliography

A Message of Hope from the Angels; Byrne, Lorna

Angels; Graham, Billy

Angels on Assignment; Buck, Rolland

Angels Walking; Kingsbury, Karen

Biblical Facts about Angels; Nicholas, Colombel

Biblical Facts about Michael the Archangel; Kranz, Jeffrey

Kingdom Quest; Jackson, Cecilia

Present Day Truths; Iverson, Dick; Scheidler, Bill

The Power of Praise and Angels; Law, Terry

What does the Bible say about Angels; Fairchild, Mary

When You Need A Miracle; Spangles, Ann

Books Published By The Authors
Drs. Michael & Cecilia Jackson

1. 9 Gifts of the Holy Spirit
2. A Synopsis: Differentiating Religion, Tradition, Church, & Kingdom
3. A Woman's Heart
4. Be Made Whole
5. Belonging
6. Beyond The Veil
7. Bold Truth
8. Breaking The Curse of Poverty
9. Get Her Back on Her Feet
10. Categorizing Spiritual Gifts
11. Dialogue Between the Watchmen and The King
12. Discern Deploy The "Heir" Force
13. Dominion For Practical Singles
14. Don't Feed The Bears
15. Finding The RIGHT Woman
16. From Press To Passion
17. Go-Forward!
18. God's Woman of Excellence For Today: The Shunammite Woman of II Kings
19. Hannah
20. It's A Wrap!
21. Kingdom Quest I
22. Make Your Valley Full of Ditches
23. Rebuilding the Economy of the Global Kingdom of God
24. Releasing The Leader Within
25. Simply Praise
26. Step Back To Sprint Forward
27. The Bible Mesmerizing, "In-Your-Face" Info
28. TRU - The Tongue of the Learned for Cultivating Racial Unity
29. Tithing Your Tithes
30. Tool Kit for Understanding Prophets and Prophetics in the Church
31. Wailing Women Warriors Win

Printed in the United States
By Bookmasters